Brother Francis

A story about Saint Francis of Assisi

written by Jan Johnson
illustrated by Kathryn E. Shoemaker

© 1977 by Winston Press, Inc.
printed in the United States of America
all rights reserved

ISBN: 0-03-022131-5
Library of Congress Catalog Card Number: 77-077684

 Winston Press 430 Oak Grove Minneapolis, MN 55403

Francis Bernadone lived a very long time ago in Italy. You may know of him as Francis of Assisi. That's because he came from the town of Assisi. (If you were named after the town you come from, what would you be called?)

People who knew Francis of Assisi told many stories about him and his work for God. Francis traveled all over Italy, talking about God's love for people and animals and all of creation. Francis loved people and animals and all of creation, too.

We still hear many stories about Saint Francis today. Maybe you know some of them.

Do you know this one?

One cold winter's night, Francis was riding his horse home from a party. Francis wore a new velvet cloak. It kept him toasty warm. As he rode along, Francis saw a poor man in the street. "Goodness," thought Francis, "that man is wearing a very thin cloak. He must be freezing. I have many more clothes than I need. I will give him my cloak."

Francis stopped the man. "Here," said Francis, removing his warm, fancy cloak. "Kind sir, would you trade cloaks with me?"

The poor man was surprised. "Well," he said, "of course I will. But why on earth would you want this raggedy cloak?"

Francis replied, "You looked so cold. And I have other cloaks. So I thought you should have a warm one, too."

"God bless you and I thank you," said the man as he went on his way.

Soon after that night, Francis decided that God wanted him to do something special with his life. He, Francis, had better find out what that was.

So, Francis walked a long way up a mountain to a small church. The church was so run-down that no one used it anymore. The brick walls were falling down. Most of the roof had blown away.

Francis went into the church to pray. He prayed
for a long time. Suddenly, he understood that God
wanted him to fix up the little church so people
could use it again.

Francis thought, "But I don't know anything
about fixing churches. Maybe I can't do what God
wants." He thought and prayed some more. "If God
wants me to fix this church, then I can," Francis
decided. "I believe God will help me."

Off Francis went to get supplies to fix the church. He bought bricks and mortar and thatching for the roof. He hauled everything back up the mountain and set to work on the church. He worked a long time. Finally the church was all repaired.

After the church was fixed, many people came there to pray and talk to God about their problems.

Francis knew what he should do next. He gave away all his clothes and money. He kept only a plain, gray robe. And he walked all over Italy telling people about God's love. He called himself "Brother Francis." When people asked why he called himself this, he said, "We are all God's children. And that makes us brothers and sisters."

Do you know the story about Brother Francis
and the birds? Well, here it is.

One day Brother Francis was walking in the
woods. Many people were following him.
These people wanted to hear about God's love
for them. So Brother Francis stopped to talk.
But the people could not hear Francis,
because the birds were singing so loudly.
(It must have been about bedtime for
the birds. You know how much noise birds
make in the evening before they go to sleep.)

Brother Francis looked up at the trees.
"Hush, little Sister Birds. Hush, little Brother
Birds," Francis said. "And I will tell a story
about God. You may listen, too. For God made
birds and loves them, too."

Suddenly the woods fell silent. And Francis
told everyone about how God takes care of all his
creatures — you and me and everything he made.

Another story tells about Brother Francis and a terrible wolf. This story took place near a town called Gubbio.

Near Gubbio lived a dangerous wolf. Some people said the wolf killed farm animals. Some said that he carried off little children. Some said that he even killed grown men and women. No one knows exactly what terrible things the wolf did. But he must have done something to make the people of Gubbio so afraid.

One afternoon Brother Francis came to Gubbio. The whole town was gathered in the village square.

Brother Francis asked a woman, "Why are you gathered here? Why do you all look so worried?"

The woman replied, "Have you not heard about the dangerous wolf? He has frightened the whole town half to death. We must decide who will go out into the forest to kill him."

"Oh," thought Francis. "The people should not kill Brother Wolf. I think he's probably hungry. I must go into the woods and talk to him. I will tell him to find his food in the woods and to leave the people alone."

Brother Francis called out to the people. "You must not kill your brother, the wolf. God made him, too. I will go into the woods to talk to Brother Wolf."

The people said, "You are crazy! You will be killed!"

But Brother Francis was not afraid. He walked into the woods alone. "Brother Wolf," Francis called, "come out and talk with me. I will not hurt you."

The fierce wolf walked right up to Brother Francis and laid down at his feet. "Brother Wolf," said Francis, "you must stop scaring the good people of Gubbio. God made you and them. He does not want you to hurt each other. You must find your food in the woods. And you must stop carrying off farm animals."

The wolf looked at Brother Francis as if to say he understood. Brother Wolf never bothered the people of Gubbio after that.

Maybe you have heard this Christmas story about Brother Francis.

Brother Francis and some other brothers walked into a town on Christmas Eve. It was quite late. Still, they expected to see people getting ready for Christmas. How surprised they were that no one was hanging any decorations. No one was getting ready to go to church.

"You know," said Francis to the brothers, "it looks to me like the people in this town have forgotten all about Christmas. They don't seem to remember that on Christmas we celebrate Jesus' birthday."

"If they don't remember Jesus' birthday, they must not know how much God loves them," replied one brother.

"You are right," said Brother Francis.
"And I have an idea about how we can remind them.
Go quickly now, Brothers. Find some tree branches
and some flowers. Find a manger. Find a donkey
and a cow. Find a mother and a father with a
new baby. Bring them all to the church. Then meet
me there at midnight."

The brothers all scurried off. They could
not imagine what Brother Francis had in mind.
But they knew he must have a reason for needing
those things. So they found them and brought them
to the church.

Meanwhile, Brother Francis went through the village knocking on doors. "Come to church at midnight," he invited. "It is Christmas. Tonight you will see something very special and very beautiful. You will see that God loves you."

Some of the people said, "What's the matter with you? Don't you know better than to knock on doors so late at night? Go away."

But Francis just replied, "God loves you. Come and see what he did for you."

And most of the people got out of their beds. They got ready to go to church. "I can't believe I'm doing this," grumbled one old man. "If God loves me, why doesn't he let me sleep?" But the grumbling man was curious like the others. So off he went to church with the rest.

When the people got to the church, this is what they saw. In front of the church was a little gateway decorated with branches and flowers. Underneath it was a man and a woman and a manger. A donkey and a cow stood next to the manger.

Brother Francis and the other brothers stood near the manger scene. They sang a song about Jesus and the first Christmas.

"What a wonderful way to celebrate," thought the people. Here was a beautiful scene to show them what it must have been like when Jesus was born. Then they remembered how much God loved them.

Everybody went into the church to thank God for sending Jesus.

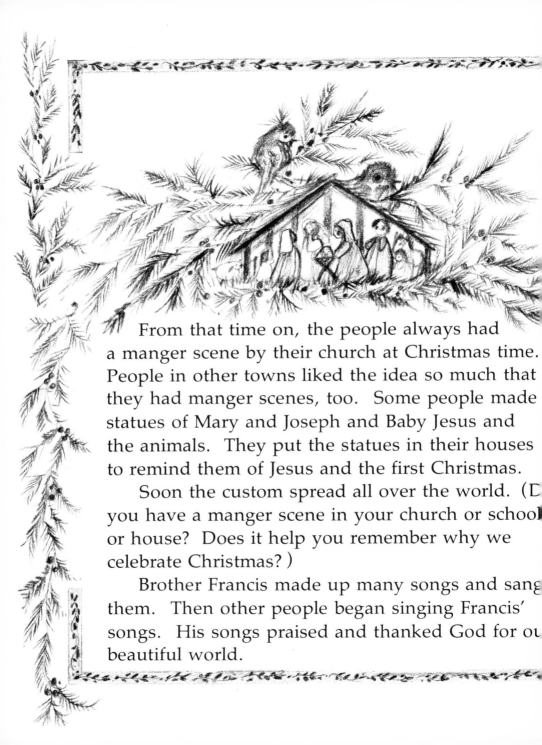

From that time on, the people always had a manger scene by their church at Christmas time. People in other towns liked the idea so much that they had manger scenes, too. Some people made statues of Mary and Joseph and Baby Jesus and the animals. They put the statues in their houses to remind them of Jesus and the first Christmas.

Soon the custom spread all over the world. (Do you have a manger scene in your church or school or house? Does it help you remember why we celebrate Christmas?)

Brother Francis made up many songs and sang them. Then other people began singing Francis' songs. His songs praised and thanked God for our beautiful world.

One of the songs we remember today goes
something like this:

> For brother sun, who brings the day
>   and gives us light,
> Be praised, my Lord.
> For sister moon and the stars,
> Be praised, my Lord.
> For brother wind,
> Be praised, my Lord.
> For sister water,
> Be praised, my Lord.
> For brother fire, who is fair
>   and happy and strong,
> Be praised, my Lord.
> For mother earth, who brings forth
>   fruit and grasses and bright flowers,
> Be praised, my Lord.
> For all your creatures,
> Be praised, my Lord.

A Biographical sketch of Francis of Assisi

Francis Bernadone was born in about 1181 to Pietro and Pica Bernadone in Assisi, Italy. Francis' father was a cloth merchant and the family was well off, though not of the nobility.

Francis devoted his life to God and has become known to all the world as Saint Francis of Assisi, lover of all God's creatures great and small. Many stories are told about him, some of them, no doubt, legendary. However, they all illustrate the simple life of a man who carried God's message of love to everyone.

It is said that when Francis was quite young he dreamed of becoming a knight or a troubador. And he is sometimes called God's troubador, because he wrote and popularized many songs, or canticles, in praise of God. The two best-known are the prayer "Lord Make Me an Instrument of Thy Peace" and the "Canticle of the Sun," which is paraphrased for young children in this book.

Francis founded the religious community for men called the Poor Brothers of Penance of Assisi, later known as Franciscans. The members owned nothing. They called themselves friars and were not ordained to the priesthood. Shortly after the founding of the Poor Brothers, Francis helped a woman named Clare organize a community for women now known as the Poor Clares.

Young children respond with delight to Saint Francis. Francis, just like all children, was filled with wonder at all of creation, and children feel a kinship with him. They especially appreciate his recognition that animals are God's creatures, too. Francis' message that we are all brothers and sisters invites them to membership in the loving family of God.